SAINT CLARE
OF ASSISI

CTS Children's Books

Contents

Text by Francesca Fabris
Illustrations by Silvia Fabris
Translated by Simone Finaldi

Saint Clare of Assisi: Published 2013 by The Incorporated Catholic Truth Society, 40-46 Harleyford Road, London SE11 5AY. Tel: 020 7640 0042; Fax: 020 7640 0046; www.cts-online.org.uk. Copyright © 2013 The Incorporated Catholic Truth Society in this English-language edition.

ISBN: 978 1 86082 848 5 CTS Code CH 46

Translated from the original Italian Edition **Santa Chiara D'Assisi** - ISBN 978-88-6124-334-7, published by Il Pozzo di Giacobbe, Gruppo Editoriale S.R.L., Cortile San Teodoro, 3, 91100 Trapani (TP), Italy © 2012 Il Pozzo di Giacobbe.

A NOBLE FAMILY

Saint Clare's family was rich and important. They lived in a beautiful house in Assisi.

Her father was Favarone Offreduccio Bernardino, one of the most powerful and respected men in the city.

Her mother's name was Ortolana and Clare loved listening to her. Ortolana would talk to Clare about God and explain the loveliest parts of the Gospels to her. So Clare grew up learning to know and love Jesus.

3

LITTLE STONES

She often wished to speak with God, especially at night, before going to sleep.

She had a little secret: to make sure she did not forget to say all her prayers, she counted them with little stones.

This is how she did it: she would kneel beside her bed, take as many stones as she could hold in the palm of her hand and lay them on the carpet.

Every time she finished a prayer, she took a stone from the carpet and put it on her bedside table. When all the stones had been moved, she had finished all her prayers.

Clare's mother was very generous. When she met a poor man on the road, she always tried to help him by giving him whatever she had.

4

Clare's mother would leave the house with a bag full of clothes and tasty things to eat, and give them to anyone begging on the street corners. She would only return home when her bag was empty.

That's how she taught Clare not to be selfish, and to care for the less fortunate. When she grew up, Clare followed her mother's example: she was good and generous to everyone. She saw no difference between the rich and the poor, because to her they were all God's children. She worked very hard to help the needy and look after the sick. Like her mother, she would leave the house with a big bag full of good food and she was happiest when she had handed everything out.

WORDS THAT CHANGED HER

One day, when she was twelve, Clare heard Saint Francis preaching. Francis stood in the middle of the town square and said loudly: "Do as I do: live in poverty! Serve Jesus in your brother! Serve him in the poor and the hungry. He needs you!" Many people passing by did not pay attention to him, but some stopped and listened because they were interested in his words. Clare was very interested too. She went home, wondering about what Francis had said.

That night she could not sleep. She tossed and turned in her bed asking herself, what could those words mean for her? What could she do? Clare already loved the Lord and served Jesus in the poor and sick every day. If she already did all this, why did the words of Francis make her think so much?

6

Only a few days before, Francis had done something incredible, that all Assisi was talking about. He had taken off all his clothes and had put them, with his saddle bag and what he had in his pockets into his father's hands, until he was completely naked.

Then he turned around towards the crowd who were watching him, astonished. He told them he preferred to live like the poor, free to be full of the love for God, instead of having lots of money and beautiful clothes. These things did not leave you free to love those most in need.

The following day Clare made a decision. She was going to go and talk to Francis.

ESCAPE IN THE NIGHT

For a while Clare regularly went to the little church of Saint Mary of the Angels. She stayed with Francis and his friends: they talked, worked and prayed together. It was wonderful!

Seven years went by and in time Clare matured. She then took the decision to live like Francis and his group of friars: poor and humble. She did not talk about this with her family, because she feared it would cause trouble and arguments: she knew her father would not be happy, but her desire was so strong that nothing could stop her.

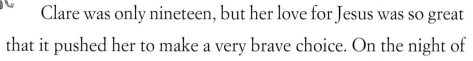

Clare was only nineteen, but her love for Jesus was so great that it pushed her to make a very brave choice. On the night of Palm Sunday in the year 1212, she ran away from her father's house, escaping secretly through a side door. She walked quickly through Assisi's dark roads, accompanied by her best friend Pacifica Guelfucci. She went to the small church of Saint Mary of the Angels, where Francis was praying while he waited for her.

9

SAINT DAMIAN

When she arrived, Francis gave her a humble brown habit to wear and covered her shoulders with a rough cloak. Then he cut her beautiful, long, curly hair and gave her a veil, which was a sign of her new life dedicated completely to God. Clare made her vows to the Lord, while Francis and the friars prayed and praised God with songs and hymns, because someone new had joined their small group.

After that night Clare stayed with the Benedictine nuns of Bastia Umbra, four kilometres from Assisi. Then she was a guest of the Benedictine monastery of Sant'Angelo. In the meantime, Francis and his friends finished the renovation of the tiny convent of Saint Damian, built next to the small church also named after Saint Damian. This became Clare's final home and the Motherhouse for her followers, who were named "Poor Clares" in her honour. Saint Clare's Order would quickly spread to all of Europe. But let's return to our story.

A PILLAR OF THE TEMPLE

When her family found out about Clare's escape, her father, her brothers and her uncle became furious; they looked for her everywhere, going up and down the streets of the city in a rage.

In the end someone revealed Clare's secret and so they rushed to the Benedictine convent. They came in roaring angrily and ran into the small chapel, where they found Clare clinging on to the altar. She had no intention of leaving. They could make all the noise they wanted, but she was going to stay.

Her father grabbed her and pulled her with all his strength, helped by his brother and his sons, but miraculously, they could not move Clare a centimetre. She was so strong that she seemed to be made of marble, a pillar holding up the Church, fixed to the ground and impossible to move.

After that, Clare's father had to accept her choice. He went back home sad and angry because he had just agreed with another nobleman from Assisi that Clare should marry a rich and powerful young man!

13

GOD'S CALLING GROWS

During this time, Clare's sisters Agnes and Beatrice stayed at home with their mother, scared of what could happen to her. They did not know anything about her new life and were very worried.

When their father and the brothers came back and told them about Clare's decision, they also wanted to follow her, the desire to join her was like a fire that made their hearts race.

Shortly afterwards, Agnes and Beatrice knocked on the convent door and asked if they could live as nuns like Clare, because they understood that the Lord was calling them to the same kind of life.

A few years later, when their father died, their mother Ortolana joined her three daughters and became a nun.

At that time, women did not go around villages and towns preaching, as Francis and the friars did; they lived at home as wives and mothers, or within the walls of a convent, as nuns.

Clare's life fascinated many other girls and ladies, who followed her in small groups: they quickly became a community of fifty people.

CLARE THE ABBESS

Such a large community needed a leader who could guide the sisters with wisdom in their daily decisions.

Francis often went to St Damian's convent and looked after the community with love, giving advice and always encouraging them. He understood that he needed to make Clare the abbess or superior, a sort of elder sister to whom everybody could turn with their questions.

The other nuns were happy to have Clare to look after them because she had such a kind heart and everybody loved her.

But the abbess also had the job of making sure that the Rule, which told them all how to live, was followed. The Poor Clares had only started a short while ago, and did not have a special Rule of their own yet.

Clare and her friends wanted to live like Francis: sharing the same poverty and humility, owning nothing, neither money nor houses nor land, living only by working and by what people gave them.

They prayed a lot for themselves and for others, they worried about the needs of everyone and offered their help to whoever asked. They wanted this to be their Rule and they asked Francis to write it down for them.

The news of her new Rule arrived in Rome and a messenger told Pope Gregory IX the story of Clare and her sisters. He was amazed to know that women, who had previously lived as rich ladies, had chosen to live a poor and difficult life because they loved Jesus.

He decided to visit them to see in person if the news was true. So Gregory IX went on a journey to the convent of St Damian.

Clare and her sisters welcomed the Pope with great joy, and served him simply and generously. Pope Gregory was very happy, but he was worried because their life was very hard.

He spoke to Clare privately, asking her to make her Rule a little less strict.

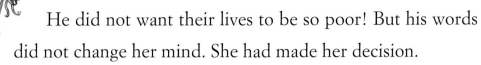

He did not want their lives to be so poor! But his words did not change her mind. She had made her decision.

She did not think the Poor Clares should live differently to Francis and his followers, just because they were women!

During dinner, the Pope asked her to bless the bread. As soon as she finished the prayer of blessing, a cross appeared miraculously on the bread. That was a sign that Clare had been right in her choice.

She asked the Pope to grant her the "Privilege of Poverty", which meant giving up everything she owned, because she felt it was the only way to follow the teachings of Jesus.

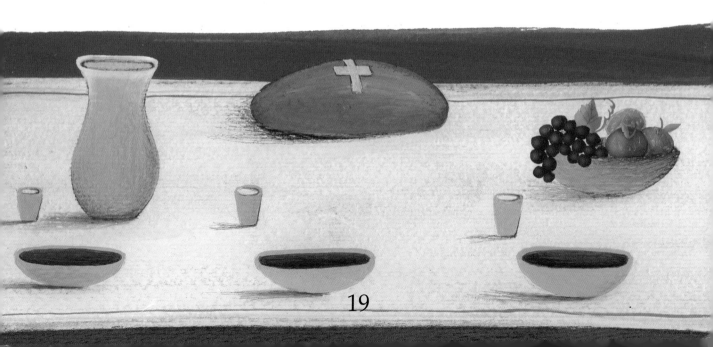

CLARE DEFENDS THE CITY

Clare lived for forty-two years in the convent of St Damian. She was very helpful and did not refuse any job, not even the most humble or unpleasant one; she carried out every task with a happy heart. Her health was rather fragile by this time: she was often ill but, despite everything, she would find the strength to get out of bed and make herself useful. Her kind words made everybody smile. She was supported by her great faith and she performed miraculous healings just by making the sign of the cross on sick people's foreheads. Once Clare was so ill she could not get up. She needed a cloth and did not know what to do. Miraculously, the convent's kitten brought her one clean and well-ironed, without creasing it.

Then came difficult times, wars and famines. Twice the city of Assisi was threatened by the emperor Frederick II of Swabia, who had many Saracen soldiers in his army.

In 1243 Clare was very ill; nevertheless, she prayed earnestly to the Lord to protect the city and the convent from the fury of the Saracens. The sisters brought her on a stretcher to the walls of the city. She had a consecrated host in her hands.

When she saw the army, Clare lifted the host and a powerful light dazzled the soldiers, who were frightened and ran away, so Assisi was safe.

PATRON SAINT OF TELEVISION

On Christmas Eve in 1252, the Franciscan friars went to celebrate Holy Mass in the church of St Damian, together with the Poor Clares.

Clare, who was very ill, had to stay in bed. She was sad and lonely in her room, really wishing she could be part of the Mass - when a miracle happened! On the wall she saw the projected images of the Mass and heard

the choir of the friars. It was like watching a modern TV! This is why she is the patron saint of television. This was the last Christmas gift Jesus gave her. Clare died on the 11th August 1253, at the age of sixty.

After only two years, the Pope proclaimed her a saint. The Church celebrates her feast day on the day of her death, the 11th August.

AN IMAGE OF SAINT CLARE

A PRAYER

Saint Clare, friend of Francis of Assisi,

friend of Jesus and of God,

you lived in poverty and believed

the words of the Gospel that say:

"Do not worry for your life,

what you are to eat or drink,

nor about your body

or what you will wear.

Your Father who is in heaven,

knows you need these things".

Teach me to follow your example

and live my life

with your faith and simplicity.

Amen.